HP

Hawkeye Publishers

The Garden Path

© Text Copyright 2022 Burton Voorhees
© Illustrations Copyright 2022 Linda Voorhees

For more information, please address Hawkeye Publishers
Los Angeles, California, USA
HawkeyePublishers.com

Library of Congress Control Number: 2022904100

Paperback: 978-1946005663
Hardcover: 978-1946005670
Ebook: 978-1946005687

The Garden Path

by Burton Voorhees

Illustrations by Linda Voorhees

"If life is a monastery, I am the monk in the garden
with a bottle of wine, singing to the moon."

With Apologies to Omar Khayyam.

I saw a Sufi sitting on a patch of ground
Heedless of belief or unbelief and all the world around.
No God, no Truth, no Divine Law, no Certitude.
Where in the two worlds is such courage found?

(adapted from the Avery and Heath-Stubbs translation of
The Ruba'iyat of Omar Khayyam: 104)

.

☆ ☆ ☆ ☆ ☆

"The Garden Path is a beautiful and unusual book. It consists of 108 illustrated limericks, a few lines of poetic inspiration dramatizing a path of spiritual liberation. The path is tricky, thorny, moving from the would-be Seekers consciousness in sleep, to uncertainty and confusion, to eventual awakening. Spiritual aspirants will find this elegant manual helpful; it can inspire as well as guide. The final section is an essay on the life and work of the medieval Persian poet Omar Khayyam, surely a fitting example of a life lived in wisdom and grace."

— Alex S. Kohav, Ph.D.

Author of The Sod Hypothesis, editor of Mysticism and Meaning and Mysticism and Experience.

☆ ☆ ☆ ☆ ☆

"Who would ever have thought that the spiritual life could be captured through a load of limericks? Not me, but I loved this little book and kept returning to it to find new meanings and deeper encouragement to practice."

— Susan Blackmore, Ph.D.

Author of Seeing Myself: What Out-of-Body Experiences Tell Us About Life, Death and the Mind; Consciousness: A Very Short Introduction; Zen and the Art of Consciousness; Ten Zen Questions; and The Meme Machine.

CONTENTS

The state of much of humanity, unaware of their true potential, seeking distraction and entertainment, frittering away real possibilities for short term gain.

The distractions of sleep pall, they no longer satisfy or entertain. Unanswered questions arise, not addressed by dogmatic answers or comforting platitudes.

Something calls, beckoning towards a path of personal realization. Initially felt as disquiet and longing for something beyond everyday life. This motivates seeking and issues a challenge.

Fantastic images of "enlightenment" attract and motivate us to investigate the reality behind mystical claims. But do we even know how to start?

We have found a group, teacher, or school that promises us progress toward some deep reward and begin to engage in the recommended practices, but remain is a state of fantasy.

Reality must be accepted before real progress can be made.

The light dawns, our path is not just some distraction or a royal road to enlightenment. It is something to be worked and understood.

Trees are known by their fruit, and we reap the fruits of our work.

As bees save honey, "workers in the vineyard" save the wisdom of humanity, passing it across generations, adapted for local conditions of time, place, and people.

We always live in dangerous times. The nature of the danger changes, but for those seeking truth one constant is the resistance and ill will of orthodoxy and fundamentalist dogma. The life of the Medieval Persian mathematician and philosopher Omar Khayyam is an example of how the essence of true seeking can be passed on without evoking the ire of fundamentalists and dogmatists.

PREFACE

A revered sage possessed a seemingly inexhaustible store of wisdom which, so it was believed, came from a thick book he kept in his chamber and was observed to consult in times of difficulty. On his death, his students rushed to obtain this book. They believed that it was their rightful possession. To their astonishment, all pages excepting the first were blank while the first page contained but a single sentence: "When you learn the difference between container and content, you will have wisdom[1]."

It is easy to know the difference between wine and bottle, far more complicated when words are the container and understanding must be pressed from them as wine is pressed from ripe grapes. Fine wine in a cheap bottle remains fine wine. Vinegar in a fancy bottle is still vinegar, even if those who judge by appearances praise it to the skies.

All that is given in experience are appearances, which can be deceiving. The name is not the thing named; the map is not the territory; the menu is not the meal. Hamlet agonizes that a person may smile, and smile, and smile, and still be a villain. The disheveled and shunned dervish Shams showed Rumi enlightenment. Appearances must be used as a bridge to the real. As the ancient saying goes, "Do not look at my outward form, take what is in my hand." The trick is to recognize whether or not what is at hand is of value. I would like to hand you this book, but doing so through proxy is a necessity of reality.

Part I of this book consists of 108 illustrated limericks, grouped into nine chapters of 12. Each limerick highlights a different aspect of a path of spiritual growth. Discerning readers will notice that the third, sixth, and ninth chapters differ from the others and that correspondingly placed limericks in each of the nine chapters can be read as a series of nine.

The nine chapters go through a sequence of life stages, beginning in Chapter 1 with a state of sleep in which a person is ignorant of their potential, fearful, caught up in the most trivial of pursuits in search of entertainment. In Chapter 2, a state of disquiet arises. The life of sleep and cheap amusement has lost its glamor, leading to confusion, uncertainty, and questioning: is this all there is? In Chapter 3, sensitivity to a spiritual calling, to beauty, to romance, and to adventure, draws a person in the direction of a meaningful path in life. But their mind remains cloaked in fantasy. Responding to this call, in Chapter 4, a person begins seeking a life path but remains mistrustful and uncertain. In Chapter 5, an inkling of a goal is sensed and a path is chosen but it is followed superficially, with little understanding, almost as a sleepwalker. Nevertheless, a foundation is being laid. Chapter 6 is a tipping point. Whatever fantasies might have motivated the initial seeking, accepting material existence is necessary to continue. Chapter 6 launches the seeker, as it were, into reality. In this sense, Chapter 7 is a repetition of Chapter 5, but now with understanding of the conditions of the chosen path. A person has become a seeker in fact as well as in name. Chapter 8 points to completion of the work, the promise of the path, the fruit by which the tree is known. Finally, Chapter 9 introduces the ancient thread of transmission, carrying the wisdom of humanity on the winds of time, uniting all humanity into a single organism.

This describes a spiritual path, but the pattern of stages adapts to fit any life path. As a youth begins to make her or his way in the world, seeking to give life meaningful content, there is uncertainty as to which path to follow. In some societies there may be an over-abundance of choices, in other societies choice is limited. Nevertheless, each life path provides a vehicle for seeking truth, finding love, and gaining wisdom. According to ancient Persian legend the cup bearer of God the Lover pours wine for God the Beloved through the symbolic forty days of life. Each life path is filled through a lifetime of living.

> This vast, unmeasured, universal vault
> Offers one bowl for all mankind to drink.
> When your turn comes, refrain from tears, be merry,
> Lift high the bowl, then drain it to its lees![2]

Part II is an essay, "Seeking Truth in Dangerous Times," illustrating aspects of a particular life path, that of the seeker of truth. The core of this essay is the balance between reason and faith, emphasizing that skepticism, in the ancient sense of the word, is perhaps the highest expression of faith. This is illustrated through the life of the Persian polymath, Omar Khayyam, who used short and seemingly blasphemous or irreligious verses to transmit a particular attitude toward the world in a time when frank and open expression could have been deadly.

PART I

THE GARDEN PATH

CHAPTER 1

ASLEEP

Prisoners in a cage of dreams,
Hypnotized by selfish schemes.
No star to light
Our path at night.
As life flows by we chase moonbeams.

THE GARDEN PATH

Dreaming life in heedless sleep,
Ducking hard work on the cheap.
Avoiding the ache
Of being awake,
Ignoring what we sow and reap.

ASLEEP

Caught in somnambulant schemes
Chasing what glitters and gleams.
With fears held at bay
I say I'm okay,
Selling my birthright for dreams.

THE GARDEN PATH

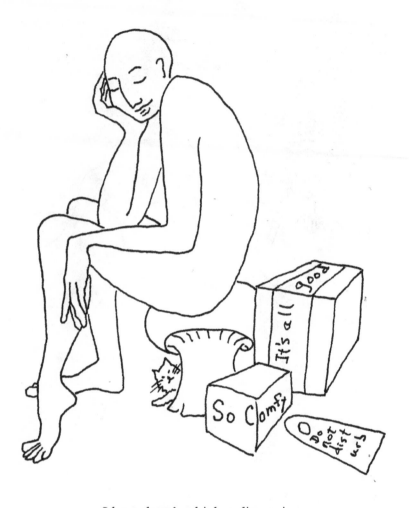

I hear there's a higher dimension,
Opening if we pay attention.
I hear the cry, Wake Up!
But I'll never shake up
Sweet fantasies' soothing pretension.

ASLEEP

Life's fatal fact won't go away
But fantasy keeps fear at bay.
In dreams I'll forget
All fright and all threat,
To wish away the livelong day.

THE GARDEN PATH

In this world of wonder, I dwell
Like a monk within his cell.
Sitting on the shelf
Lying to myself,
A hermit crab stuck in a shell.

ASLEEP

God breathes life into our clay,
Sees the meanings when we pray.
Believing we've reached him
We've only impeached him,
Preaching our dreams as His way.

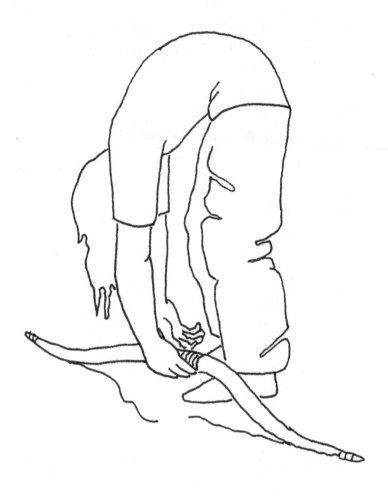

There was a time, not long ago,
When I felt free of times swift flow.
I sought wealth and fame,
Then tomorrow came.
Alas, the arrow'd left the bow.

Some who died before our time
Dreamt dreams magnificent, sublime.
But they never expressed
The love in their breast—
Their corpses are not worth a dime.

See sparkling personalities
Waving banners in each breeze.
Parading in style
They glitter and smile,
Proud of their dreadful disease.

ASLEEP

I do not want to know what's true,
I know enough to get me through.
I need no instruction,
No ego-reduction,
The world owes me, no duty's due.

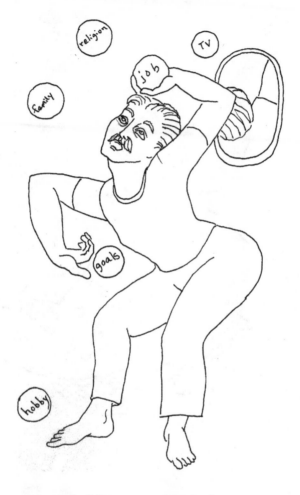

Of all I want, nothing's clearer
Then dodging fear as death comes nearer.
With quick mindless actions
And fancy distractions
I'll never look into that mirror.

CHAPTER 2

UNCERTAINTY AND CONFUSION

The end of time's our final breath,
The wise advise, die before death.
So, tell me dear friend,
When facing that end,
Will you buy a happy myth?

Striving to decide what's true,
What's right, what's wrong, what is our due?
What's God's true intent?
Are ills Heaven sent?
There may be light, but I've no clue.

With seductive tales of a prize,
A succulent feast greets my eyes.
These tellers of tales
Chalk up their sales
Peddling sugary lies.

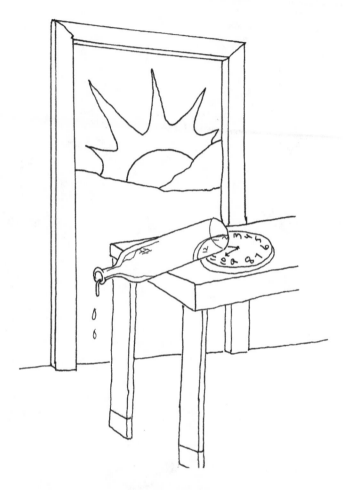

Life's sparkling wine is poured and gone,
No promise of a second dawn.
Must I walk alone
Into that unknown,
Without a friend to lean upon?

UNCERTAINTY AND CONFUSION

Sorting chaff to find the wheat,
Seeking in each face I meet
A guide I can trust
To burnish the rust...
Can I be trusted not to cheat?

THE GARDEN PATH

Those who tell us what and why
Spin changing tunes as moons go by.
But one thing is certain,
Life's final curtain
Falls for all and that's no lie.

UNCERTAINTY AND CONFUSION

False fantasies inside my head,
Wandering as they are led
By desires and fear,
By tales that I hear—
In mindless chatter, fears are bred.

THE GARDEN PATH

On the brink of the abyss,
Dancing betwixt that and this,
Pulled here and there,
Each side a snare.
Will wonder lead me on to bliss?

UNCERTAINTY AND CONFUSION

We've found the secrets of the Potter,
Gained wisdom from Heaven's Daughter.
In spite of all gains
The question remains,
Are we lambs for the slaughter?

The bird in the ribcage must fly,
But fearful of making a try,
Safe in its cage
It waits for a mage
Whose magic will open the sky.

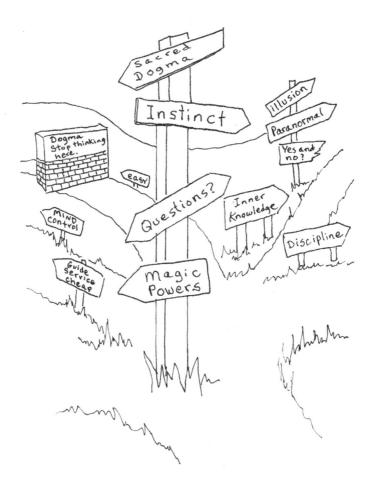

Occult mysteries lead astray,
Sacred dogma's not the way.
Is there a way clear
Beyond greed and fear,
Sliding between yea and nay?

THE GARDEN PATH

Two roads in a dark woodland,
To Mecca, or to Samarkand?
In such a dark wood
I would that I could
See one to the Promised Land.

CHAPTER 3

The Calling

Something's calling, day and night.
Our Spirit, yearning to take flight
Acts as a goad
To follow that road.
Attend the teacher—travel light.

In my heart's an unknown need,
A ripening irritant and seed.
My Northern Star
Calls from afar,
To follow on where it may lead.

THE CALLING

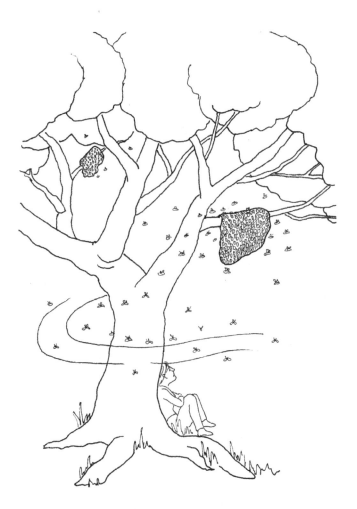

Her call sighs softly on the breeze.
A teasing whisper in the trees
Says honey awaits
My date with the fates,
Oh sweet, sweet possibilities.

I saw believers in a trance,
Yelled out, Wake Up! Take a chance!
Not seeing a need
Myself to be freed,
From slumbering in sleeps' romance.

THE CALLING

I hear the piper on the hill
Play Orphic airs that raise a chill.
Her wild wine song
Sweeps me along
With mystic visions of what's real.

Whispered tales in darkest night
Bring hope, or leave us in a fright.
So tell me I'm fine,
Pour me sweet wine,
Promise me sweetness and light.

THE CALLING

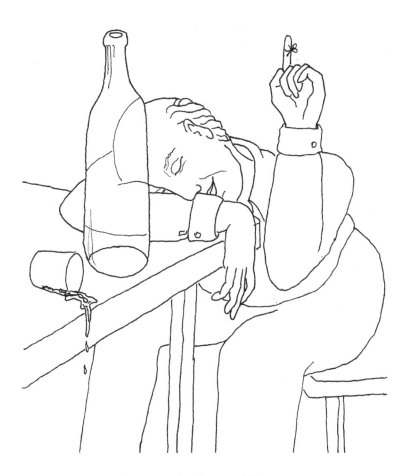

A scary tale if you will hear,
A song to coax compassion's tear.
The struggle and pain
Of life lived in vain…
Share our wine and banish fear.

A song will get us through the night,
A song will prep us for a fight.
As troops march along
They're singing that song,
A song can sing us to the light.

THE CALLING

Nature molds us on her wheel,
Casts illusions we call real.
When we understand her
We'll surely command her,
On this, science is the seal.

THE GARDEN PATH

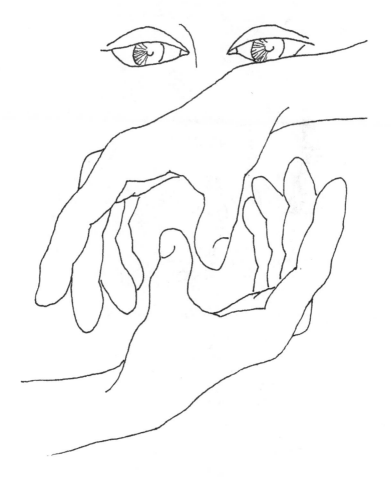

I met a man reputed wise,
Heard his words, tried them for size.
I waffled a bit
But knew that they fit,
Looking deeply in his eyes.

THE CALLING

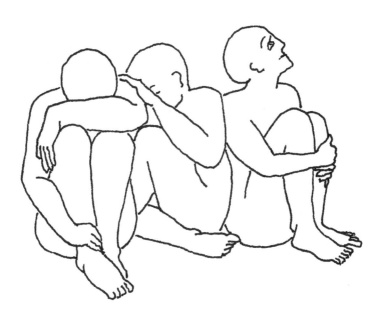

See those folks who dream in slumber?
Long I've slept among their number.
The Guide cries Awake!
There's a journey to take!
Drop all burdens that encumber.

THE GARDEN PATH

This path was mapped out long ago
With road marks set by those who know.
Cast off cruel sleep
We've a promise to keep,
We're called to fight an ancient foe.

CHAPTER 4

SEEKING A PATH

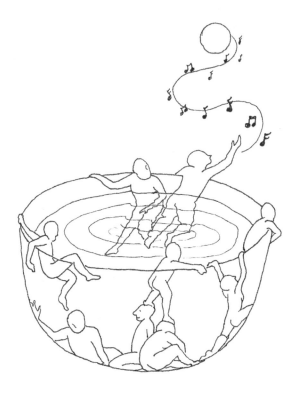

Flung into this mixing bowl
Where time and chance extract their toll.
Tumbling about
In a cauldron of doubt,
Seeking the Celestial Pole.

THE GARDEN PATH

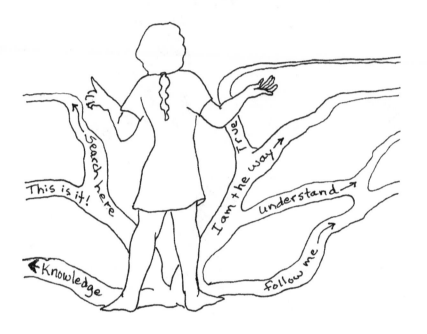

In this labyrinth, no clue,
I need a guide to see me through.
Beginnings call out
Try this or that route…,
I want an accurate preview.

SEEKING A PATH

I sought out educated guys
For answers to the how's and why's.
Much talk of this and that
But none stepped up to bat,
Or shared the secrets of the wise.

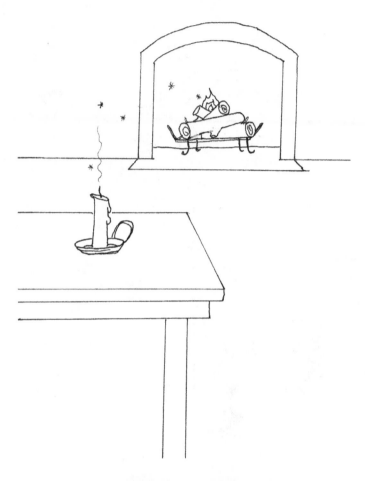

The brightest flame will flicker low,
Hearth embers may lose their glow.
But a single spark
Can kindle the dark,
As light for those who seek to know.

SEEKING A PATH

Throw worldly cares to the breeze,
True wonder sets Spirit at ease.
And what could go wrong
Not fixed by a song?
All flowers give honey to bees.

THE GARDEN PATH

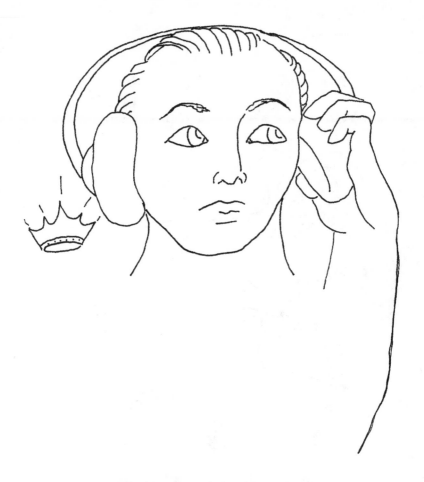

The Teacher of the Age is near
Imparting wisdom, bright and clear.
What we see's the bit
That we think will fit,
We hear what we're prepared to hear.

SEEKING A PATH

Siren songs ring in my mind
Spinning tales of wealth to find.
I'm looking to see
What's best for me,
But hot desire leaves me blind.

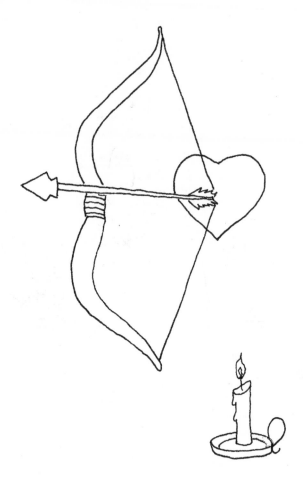

A glimpse of light may be a clue
For aspiration to aim true.
When drawing the bow
There's one thing to know—
The heart's true compass sees us through.

Counting mistakes that I've made
Reckoning costs that I've paid.
If I am reborn
I'll be most forlorn
Should memory not offer me aid.

It's bozos on the bus we are,
Gathering from near and far.
This circus goes on
From dusk until dawn,
And every one of us a Star.

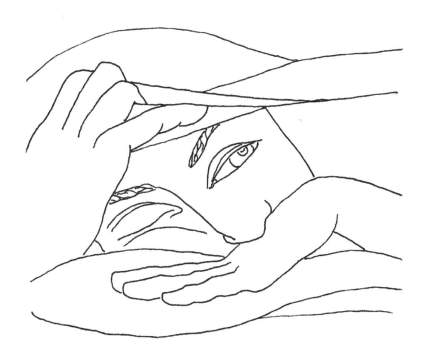

The law says as we sow, we reap
And wisdom's cost is never cheap.
The opening door
That promises more,
Acknowledging "I Am Asleep."

THE GARDEN PATH

The breeze born scent of rose is sweet,
But hungry folk must also eat.
When beggars are starving
They don't care who's carving.
We've caught the scent, let's find the meat.

CHAPTER 5

THE WORK OF
THE PATH

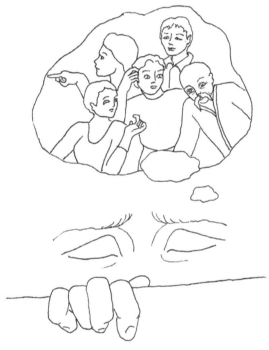

In this dream I'll work to wake,
With hope hypnotic spells will break.
With work I'll unbind
The knots of my mind,
Learning what's real and what's fake.

An irritation in a shell
Is woven in a magic spell.
Caught in the whirl
Of making a pearl,
We spin upon that carousel.

THE WORK OF THE PATH

Working to attain the goal
Becoming human, free and whole.
However we see it
We're seeking to be it,
Dreaming of our fated role.

THE GARDEN PATH

Learning from errors long past,
Seeing with whom I'd been cast.
All of those folk
I once thought a joke,
Now teachers and gurus at last.

THE WORK OF THE PATH

Seeking truth, I reached a door
That long-time seekers stood before.
In wonder they chatted
But none would get at it.
Striding up, I asked for more.

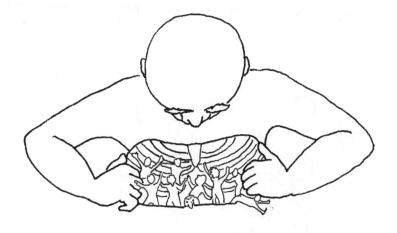

Inside I saw a multitude,
And every one demanding food.
Is there Unity,
A one truly Me,
Beyond this madly hungry brood?

THE WORK OF THE PATH

Pressed by the past a plan is laid
With hope the future sees us paid.
Shun greedy confusion!
Drop that illusion!
Past is gone, future's not made.

THE GARDEN PATH

No arrow changes once in flight.
The target's there, did I aim right?
As charioteer
I'll cheerfully steer,
In faith this road leads to the light.

THE WORK OF THE PATH

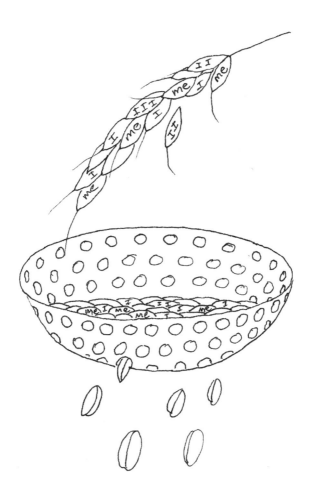

The world surrounds us as we live,
What royal treasures it can give!
Avoiding conceit
Cull chaff from the wheat,
With your conscience as a sieve.

THE GARDEN PATH

Drunkards come and drunkards go
Sampling wines that vintners show.
It's fine to get sauced
But reckon the cost,
Wine shows truth, as we well know.

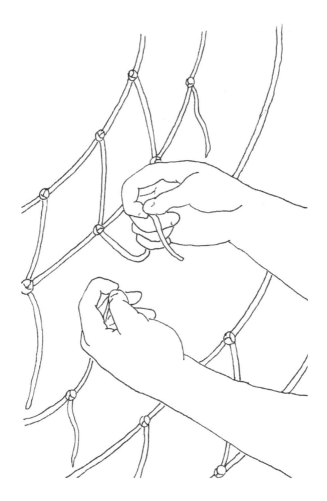

Dropping ideas, feelings, thought,
Beliefs that over time we've bought.
For mind to be quiet
We've got to untie it,
Not knit the knots that keep it caught.

THE GARDEN PATH

Raise a cup to waiting lip
Drink a toast to fellowship.
Sweet wines of love
That flow from above,
Bring joy to our companionship.

CHAPTER 6

ACCEPTING EXISTENCE

Our time for living in the Sun
Is short and swift, then time is done.
With nothing to fear
Before we were here,
Why fear returning to the One.

THE GARDEN PATH

For those who say we live in vain,
Life's only suffering and pain.
They don't see the joy
Of a boy with a toy,
Or lovers in a summer rain.

A seed puts forth a shoot and grows,
With hopes to be a red, red rose.
But not every blossom
Can be so awesome,
A daisy's pretty…, I suppose.

Each drop of wine spilt without care
Some soul may find an answered prayer.
A casual remark
Could be a bright spark
To salve a grieving soul's nightmare.

ACCEPTING EXISTENCE

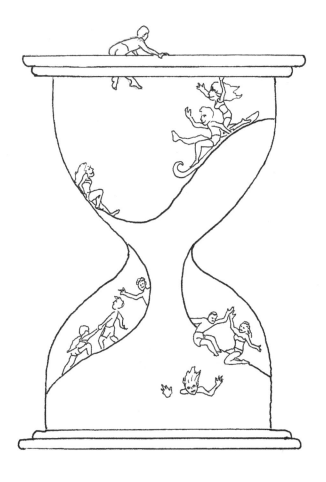

Knowing that we pass away
Opens doors to love and play.
Come sit with the friends,
Let's make our amends,
Travelling toward the dawning day.

THE GARDEN PATH

At times, attending to the Guide,
I stumbled, stopped, and sought to hide.
As effort expands
We need helping hands,
So here the gravest sin is pride.

ACCEPTING EXISTENCE

The end of time waits in the wings,
An end to all that living brings.
When winds blow away
All we've had to say,
We're one with beggars, whores, and kings.

THE GARDEN PATH

The teacher can't show us our place,
Or save us from the fate we face.
But what we can learn
Quells all concern,
Fills life with gratitude and grace.

ACCEPTING EXISTENCE

Some say religion is the way,
It's only science, others say.
But flowers don't care
What perfumes they share
And freely turn to face the day.

God's in heaven, we're on Earth,
The elderly die, young women give birth.
We're spinning around
On this Merry-Go-Round,
Singing with laughter and mirth.

ACCEPTING EXISTENCE

Tied to a chariot, dogs come along,
No choices, no matter how strong.
By reality bound
Our freedom is found,
Singing our verse in life's song.

THE GARDEN PATH

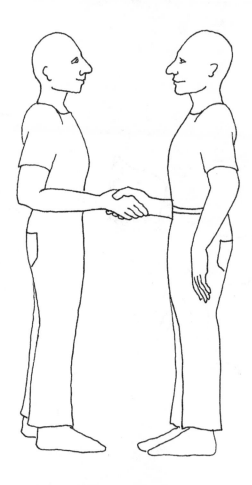

Sifting memories brought to shrive,
Exorcizing ghosts that live
As guilt and regret
For each unpaid debt—
For freedom, self must self forgive.

CHAPTER 7

AWAKENING TO THE PATH

In dim and distant days of youth
I styled myself a mystic sleuth.
But truths that I sought
Were not what I got.
It's time to learn to live in truth.

A single inch is not a mile,
A grain of sand is not a pile.
Each instant of life
Cuts time like a knife.
Taking all together, smile.

Life today seems so mundane,
Brief pleasure, boredom, troubles, pain.
But as they unfold
It's really all gold,
Each instant is a gate to gain.

With time and work we learn to play
The instruments that earn our pay.
The greatest technique
Is just a dry creek,
Its Spirit flies beyond foreplay.

We're drinking from a fragile bowl,
Crafted for its unique role.
When each day we're lent's
A full day well spent,
Why wonder when the bell will toll.

THE GARDEN PATH

In the practice of this School,
We need to heed a simple rule.
The Work that we do
Will carry us through
And gift us with a precious jewel.

An instant's loss may turn to gain,
Or seed life with regret and pain.
Acceptance's the way
To joy on that day.
Be true, don't excuse or explain.

THE GARDEN PATH

Along this path there is a state
Where gods and angels hesitate.
But songs on the breeze
Set stout hearts at ease
And lift them to a joyous fate.

AWAKENING TO THE PATH

Wounded by the world's wear,
Weary warriors, worn threadbare.
We do what we can
For our fellow man,
Working to bear our fair share.

The heart contains a shining spark
Lighting our way through the dark.
Then dawn until dusk
With body as husk,
The Sun God sails a golden barque.

AWAKENING TO THE PATH

With gratitude I'll greet each day
Knowing time is short for play.
So, while I'm still here
I'll hold my time dear,
And like a potter, shape my clay.

THE GARDEN PATH

When taking leave of our parade
A friend from life comes to your aid.
So be of good cheer,
Your best friend is near,
All karmic debts are finally paid.

CHAPTER 8

PROMISE AND COMPLETION OF THE PATH

Reality is so diverse,
Each atom of this universe
Sheds illumination
On every station,
As silent light shines on this verse.

THE GARDEN PATH

Those most perfect of our kind,
Will o'er leap all the ties that bind.
Studying essence
They find quintessence,
The empty center of their mind.

A dead man walking came my way.
I asked him, Sir, what do you say?
He gave a quick grin
And said, it's no sin
To laugh and to dance and to play.

THE GARDEN PATH

Veils fell from my mind's eye
And with this fall, the loss of "I."
The world was there,
...I was nowhere.
A bell rings in the empty sky.

As I wander on my way
Be good they say, there's Hell to pay.
But outshining this
Are wonder and bliss.
True wonder is the way to pray.

A finger pointing at the Moon,
Reasons task and reasons boon.
A guiding light
Through darkest night,
Heralding Sunrise is soon.

Those goods for which we have been vying
Lose value when we see we're dying.
It's when we get old
We find the real gold's
The One we've become in the trying.

THE GARDEN PATH

That world created in our mind,
Someday we'll leave it all behind.
Who is it will say,
On that fateful day,
This world is Good, with love aligned.

PROMISE AND COMPLETION OF THE PATH

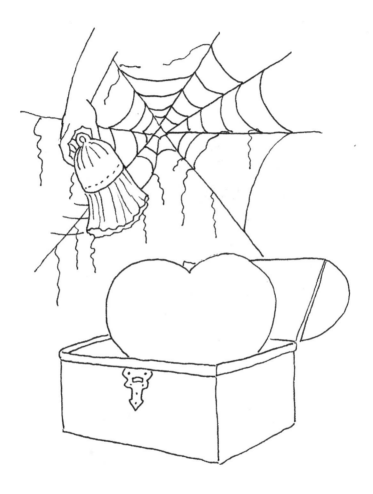

Without the manacles of thought,
Those woven webs where hearts are caught.
The Spirit remains
Enriched by our gains,
And hard lessons the heart's been taught.

THE GARDEN PATH

We're still just bozos on this bus,
We laugh and cry, we fight and cuss.
But if we're adapt
And learn to accept,
All worries are superfluous.

Whatever lot is mine today
I'll treat it as a potter's clay.
I'll shape it with art
For when I depart,
From that cup I'll drink my pay.

We dance and sing in sweet delight
Wending homeward through the night.
At end of the day
What scene's left to play
Save toasting the gift of the light.

CHAPTER 9

THE ETERNAL SCHOOL

The image of eternity
Will move between us, you and me,
But a sensitive mind
Will find, if inclined,
A ship to sail this endless sea.

THE GARDEN PATH

Our teacher taught us what to know
For rising from this world below.
You wonder, dear friends,
How this story ends?
Like water on the wind we go.

THE ETERNAL SCHOOL

Dry sands drink a river's flow,
Those sparkling waters once were snow.
Now, that journey's done.
Raised by the Sun,
It's swiftly with the wind they go.

THE GARDEN PATH

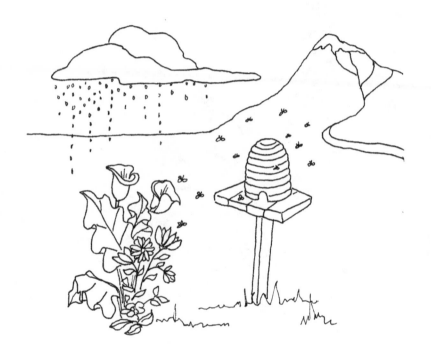

Falling rain in soft spring showers
Brings new life to budding flowers.
And bees as collectors
Accumulate nectars,
Honey saved for urgent hours.

Breeze-born perfumes from the past,
Past flowers' scents to breezes cast.
Struck by a spark
They'll shine in the dark
As lanterns hanging on our mast.

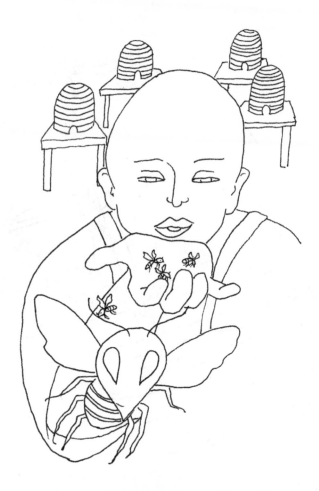

We save the best, as best we know,
Keeping it where it can grow.
Like our friends, the bees
We harvest the breeze,
Save honey from the ancient foe.

THE ETERNAL SCHOOL

Save what we can, the duty's clear,
Lose what we must, though it be dear.
Adapting our rhyme
To people and time,
Steering toward a distant pier.

THE GARDEN PATH

Great past masters of design
Planted grapes we press for wine.
They did what they could
To establish the Good,
It's up to us to tend the vine.

THE ETERNAL SCHOOL

The Potter casts fate on the breeze,
We're the ones who seek the keys.
There's dust on the wheel
From what once was real,
As potters throw new pots to please.

THE GARDEN PATH

From those before us at this table,
Remembrances, as they were able.
Though we joke and jest
It's no time to rest,
Duty calls to tell the fable.

THE GARDEN PATH

"The adventure of the mystical philosopher
is essentially a voyage
which progresses towards the light."
— Henri Corbin
(1998: 140) The Voyage and the Messenger.

THE ETERNAL SCHOOL

In every time the Truth is One,
The Song of how a life is spun.
Teaching true keys
To harvest the breeze,
Sailing for the sovereign Sun.

We're doing our best to impart
The Truth that's been known from the start.
When all's said and done
Humanity's One—
We're one with that One in our Heart.

Part II

Seeking Tr
in Dangerous 1

> You traders on God's bounty, show
> Us how to gain it, if you know.
> Stop shooting the breeze,
> Show the way, please,
> Our camels are loaded, we're ready to go.

Seekers of Truth

Plato's dialogue, "The Symposium," is set at a dinner party. In ancient Athens, these parties were overseen by a captain who decided two things: the topic of conversation, and how much water to mix with the wine. In other words, what would be discussed, and how drunk the speakers would be. Much water was mixed with the wine at this party. Many of those present were already hungover and had no desire for further indulgence. It was to be a sober discussion. The topic of conversation was love. Prominent Athenians spoke of this mysterious power, with Socrates the last to speak. Rather than speak for himself, however, Socrates relates what he had been told by the priestess Diotima. In the male dominated world of ancient Athens, a woman speaking through Socrates is a powerful statement.

Diotima speaks of beauty, how love of beauty leads a person to become a seeker of truth, rising across an ascending scale beginning with beauty in nature, then in fellow humans, and finally in wisdom and truth. She tells Socrates that neither the gods nor the ignorant[3] seek wisdom. The gods are already wise, and who seeks for what they already possess. The ignorant are self-satisfied, with no desire to seek anything beyond the pleasures of ordinary life. Who then, Socrates asked, are the seekers of truth? Diotima replied that they are those between who, knowing that they lack wisdom and have not found truth, continue seeking, drawn on by love.

This is important, wisdom and truth are sought because of attraction. Seekers of truth are not driven by emotions such as greed or fear, they are attracted by love of beauty—in nature, in fellow humans, and in wisdom. A century later, Aristotle wrote that people come to philosophy out of wonder. Philosophy, philia-Sophia is, literally, love of wisdom. Greek, however, has different words for different flavors of love. Philia refers to love as friendship, companionship. Philosophers are friends of wisdom. They may feel the erotic power of eros, but if this is not tempered by friendship, they get into trouble[4].

The Roman philosopher, Sextus Empiricus, may have been inspired by the Symposium when, some six hundred years later, he described three schools of philosophy: dogmatists, who believed their doctrines were the truth; academics (relativists), who denied the existence of truth; and skeptics, who, suspending judgment, neither affirm nor deny but continuing to seek.

In a rude characterization; for dogmatists, friendly love has fallen into possessive idolatry while relativists scorn their lover as an unfaithful harlot, telling seductive tales to all who pay her fee. Only skeptics remain orientated toward truth without becoming possessive of it, or denying its possibility. As a friend of wisdom, a skeptic knows it is not wise to proclaim any system as final truth, or to assert that there is no truth to be found. Standing between dogma and doubt a skeptic uses both, when necessary, as tools. Every inquiry needs a foundation to stand upon and a questioning attitude to prevent that floor from becoming a ceiling.

In religion, Sextus' classification carries over to dogmatic religionists insisting that their creed is ultimate truth; atheists, denying anything beyond material existence; and agnostic skeptics who, having rejected both atheism and dogmatism, continue to seek.

People think in terms of opposites, so skeptics are often counted as atheists but an honest skeptic cannot be an atheist. Who would bother seeking what they did not acknowledge might exist? The skeptic navigates a middle way between the clashing rocks of dogma and the whirlpools of doubt, treating proclamations of ultimate truth as at best signposts along the way and at worst as chains binding the mind, fettering reason, and confining the soul.

The Name and The Named

It would be a lie to say that the title of this book is a hat tip to The Walled Garden of Truth by the medieval Persian poet, Hakim Sanai, or even to the famous painting The Garden of Earthly Delight by Hieronymus Bosch. Its inspiration is from the Ruba'iyyat of Omar Khayyam. The naming took place on a sunny spring afternoon as the author sat in a coffee shop in Victoria, British Columbia, watching people and drinking

English Breakfast tea. Flowers were blooming and trees were budding, creating a garden-like atmosphere. I remembered that *Paradise* comes from *Pardis,* which is the Persian word for garden. The phrase "to lead one up the garden path" popped into mind, and a twist of humor led to the title. All of us, in one way or another, are being led along a garden path.

Khayyam entered my life shortly after returning from eighteen months teaching physics and mathematics at a private college in Tehran, Iran. There I had developed an interest in Sufism, sparked by a debate with a student of Sufism carried out in the opinion columns of the Tehran Journal, the local English Language newspaper. On returning home this interest was stoked by reading Idries Shah's book The Sufis, where Khayyam is presented as a Sufi exemplar. I found the Ruba'iyyat fascinating and it became a lifetime companion. Khayyam was an honest skeptic and the story of his life is an example of what it means to live that path.

A garden path is a path that leads to and through a garden. Perhaps a garden of truth, perhaps not. A walled garden, though, within which one finds manicured grasses, ponds with lily pads where koi and other fish swim, flowering shrubs, bushes, fruit bearing trees. Bees and butterflies visit blossoming flowers. Perhaps there is an aviary with bright colored birds and a few peacocks strutting about. It is a place where a person can wander enjoy the beauties of nature, become lost in thought, meditation, contemplation, appreciation. There are hidden glades where lovers can tryst.

SEEKING TRUTH IN DANGEROUS TIMES

Ancient Stoic philosophers compared philosophy to a garden, with logic as the walls, natural philosophy (science) as the trees, and ethics as the fruit. Epicurus, founder of the Epicurean School of philosophy, located his school, "The Garden," in a garden he purchased in Athens. In Abrahamic religious scripture, Adam and Eve lived innocently in freedom in the Garden of Eden until they were tempted by a serpent.

Gardens evoke powerful images of peace, innocence, and tranquility. They are a refuge, taking the mind away from the hustle and hurry of daily life. A garden is a place to relax, regain equanimity, stroll about in appreciation amidst greenery, fountains, and flowers. A place to take a lover, sit by a pond, discuss philosophy, read verses from the Ruba'iyyat, engage in playful seductions—so long as serpents are avoided.

Khayyam's verses provoke thought; they undermine belief and dogma, ask deep theological and metaphysical questions, equally challenging both dogmatism and relativism, accepting no easy answers. A medieval Islamic commentator wrote, "His poems are like snakes who bite the shari'ah and are chains and handcuffs on religion.[5]"

Leading a person up or down the garden path is a euphemistic way of saying that one is deceiving them. Many young innocents have (often willingly) lost their virginity (physical or metaphysical) as they were led up (or down) a garden path by smooth talking seducers. Willingness to undertake adventure, trepidation at imagined possibilities, recitations of romantic poetry, the scent of flowers blooming in the spring, these elements of set and setting work miracles.

> A loaf of bread beneath the bending bow,
> A flask of wine, a book of verse, and Thou
> Beside me, singing in the wilderness—
> Ah, wilderness were paradise enow.[6]

Living in Dangerous Times

It's dangerous to be a skeptic—questioning accepted authorities can be deadly. When fundamentalists control society they suppress dissenting voices, especially skeptics. The instinct to think in terms of us versus them applies not only to unbelievers but even more strongly to those who appear non-committal. The infidel is known and can be dealt with. Skeptics are dangerous, disruptive, untrustworthy. They encourage people to think, to ask embarrassing questions. Allow them a voice and they will subvert the social order.

In dangerous times, deviant thoughts are best expressed through channels that are not taken seriously by the orthodox, equivocating with language that can support multiple meanings. Humor is a great vehicle. Dogmatists notoriously lack a sense of humor and will see at most a single meaning in a joke. Art in all forms is effective, too. Omar Khayyam wrote short four-line verses (ruba'i) expressing views that if spoken directly would have branded him heretic. A dogmatic listener, hearing them expressed as a casual verse, could smile and give a prepackaged answer, assuming that Khayyam was feeding him a straight line rather than questioning the foundations of his entire belief system. A less blinkered listener would see the sting in the verse, be provoked to thought, perhaps repeat the verse later.

In Khayyam's lifetime, questioning Islam was punishable by death. Today, there is greater latitude for opinion. Religion is socially influential, but it has lost its life and death grip, and it struggles to remain relevant in a materialistic world of scientism and postmodern sophistry. The old dichotomy of dogma and doubt wears a new guise: those who believe that all truth is given by science, and those who claim that there is no truth other than what is politically useful. Worshippers at the altar of scientism believe science is complete, rather than a work in progress. Postmodern relativists claim that all knowledge is relative, ultimately grounded in nothing other than power and privilege. It's all idle talk, to be manipulated by the most persuasive speaker for personal or ideological gain.

Opposed in fundamental ways, scientific dogmatists and modern-day sophists agree on one thing—materialism. A side-effect of the rise of empirical science in the eighteenth-century Age of Enlightenment was loss of the "vertical dimension" of human consciousness. The gnostic idea of "vertical ascent" morphed into the ideal of a utopian future to be brought about by science[7]. The only way to discuss consciousness, mind, and spirit in a materialist setting is as things that somehow emerges from matter.

This book is not inimical to science, or to the purported open-minded tolerance of relativism, but science needs to extend beyond materialism and relativism needs to be curbed by understanding the difference between rhetoric and reality. The verses in Part I are structured by the vertical ascent, the path laid out by Diotima over twenty-four hundred years ago.

The Big Tent

A ruba'i is a four-line verse in which the first, second, and fourth lines rhyme. This was a popular poetic form in medieval Persia as a way of making short, snappy, pointed statements. Many parallels exist between limericks and ruba'i. As with ruba'i, limericks are short, pithy, outside the formal literary canon, used to mock establishment rules or social customs. They are often naughty and if the third and fourth lines of a limerick are collapsed to a single line, they follow the ruba'i rhyming scheme with the addition of an internal rhyme in the third line.

Ruba'i today, although composed by many as terse, compact statements designed to provoke, mock, amuse, or seduce are almost always associated with Khayyam's Ruba'iyyat. Over 1400 ruba'i go under Khayyam's name. Khayyam means "tent maker" and his Ruba'iyyat spreads a big tent. Published versions of the Ruba'iyyat, however, run from one hundred to about three hundred verses, those that experts believe are most likely to be authentic. Khayyam has become the exemplar of a way of thinking, expressed through his Ruba'iyyat, through his metaphysical writings, and by the example of his life. He was an honest seeker of truth, and by learning something about his life we learn something about the vicissitudes of that path.

Omar Khayyam (1048 – 1131) was born and lived most of his life in Nishapur, a city of Northeastern Persia. Nishapur was a center of Persian intellectual and religious life and capitol of the province of Khurasan. Located strategically on the Silk Road between China and the West it was a wealthy commercial center, often fought over by contending conquerors. In Khayyam's lifetime Khurasan was controlled by the Turkish Saljuq dynasty. Persians are proud people and resentment at being ruled by Turks fed an undercurrent of Persian nationalism. Ninety years later Nishapur was destroyed and its citizens butchered by the army of Genghis Khan.

In Khayyam's time, unlike the relative permissiveness of earlier centuries, Persian social and religious life was dominated by a strict interpretation of Islam. Professor Mehdi Aminrazavi describes the intellectual atmosphere in which Khayyam found himself: "Shari'ah had become the supreme truth, and formalism was identified with faith; orthodox jurists... had established their hegemony and the era of free thinking had effectively come to an end[8]."

Khayyam, on the other hand, is thought of as a free thinker, perhaps even an atheist. In his day, he was never accused of atheism although in his youth suspicions were raised which he allayed, or perhaps escaped, by making the pilgrimage to Mecca. During his lifetime, his reputation remained untarnished, and by middle age, he was honored as the preeminent scientist, mathematician, and philosopher of his day, hailed as a master of Quranic interpretation, called guardian of the substance of prophecy by the great Sufi poet Hakim Sanai.

In the centuries following Khayyam's death, however, questions arose. Opinions polarized between those who saw him as a free-thinking heretic and those who claimed him as a Sufi mystic. His scientific and philosophical works stood firmly within the accepted canons of his day. Had he stuck to that he would be remembered as the scientific and philosophical giant that he was, but he also wrote irreverent verses. Contemporaries spoke highly of his poetry, but they did not think of him as a poet and no collection of his verses was published during his lifetime. This may have saved him from scandal—the Ruba'iyyat not only transgresses orthodoxy, it obliterates it.

Khayyam's ruba'i were more than just random verses. They represented "an intellectual response to the rise of religious dogmatism, an endeavor to question and deconstruct a faith-based dogmatic theology that stifled rationalism and creativity.[9]" He got away with this because short verses exchanged among friends can be excused. Even if apparently heretical, they can be overlooked, as when a person farts in a gathering of the elite. If the person is a lowly peasant this is only expected; if they are one of the elites, the faux pas is politely ignored. As a prominent member of the court of several Sultans, Khayyam was adept at survival in court politics. Among other skills, this requires being careful not to give indication of holding beliefs that might arouse suspicion of political or religious unorthodoxy.

Through ruba'i, Khayyam found a way to express doubts, question authority, and make provocative statements without suffering the wrath of the guardians of all that is right and proper. More daring individuals, such as Mansur al Hallaj and Shihab al Din Shurawardi, were not so fortunate—they were tortured and executed as heretics.

Khayyam was well aware of the dire fate awaiting those who strayed too far from the party line and he acted accordingly to preserve his independence, not to mention his health.

> The secrets which my book of love has bred,
> Cannot be told for fear of loss of head;
> Since none is fit to learn, or cares to know,
> 'Tis better all my thoughts remain unsaid.[10]

Was Khayyam a Sufi?

Omar Khayyam, respected as the greatest scientist of his age, esteemed philosopher, master of Quranic studies, friend of Sultans, was also the theologically down and dirty Khayyam who wrote verses challenging religious belief, questioning God, apparently denying that the meaning of life was anything other than eating, drinking, and making merry. Some scholars, unable to resolve this conundrum, suggest that there were two Khayyam's, the one who wrote brilliant treatises on mathematics, metaphysics, and astronomy, and another disreputable Khayyam who wrote the Ruba'iyyat. How could this apparent contradiction exist in the same person? How is it possible to assimilate such different facets of behavior in a single character?

As a mathematician and astronomer Khayyam made substantial contributions, including ground breaking work on geometric solutions of cubic equations and development of a calendar of such accuracy that it is used in Persia today. His fame in the West, however, began in the nineteenth century when Edward Fitzgerald published a rather free translation of some verses from the Ruba'iyyat. To the socially constrained Victorian mind, these seemed to extol a hedonistic life of pleasure and disbelief, to be cynical, pessimistic about human hopes and possibilities, and critical of the creator.

The Victorian world cast Khayyam as a free-thinking rebel, chaffing under the oppression of Islamic law. And his verses can be read under that interpretation. From another view, however, they can be read as playing on themes and images used by Sufi mystics. Even so, there is controversy. Some Sufis have claimed the Ruba'iyyat as a powerful expression of Sufi thought, others have denounced it as heretical and atheistic. Khayyam was certainly well versed in Sufism. One of his most famous lines is the fourth line in the verse

> In childhood once we crouched before our teacher,
> Growing content in time with what he taught;
> How does the story end? What happened to us?
> We came like water and like wind were gone.[11]

This is a great verse, speaking to the angst of passing time. The initial two lines suggest the comfort and safety of dogmatic belief. We come into life, we are taught comforting lessons, and our mind flows like water into the forms given to us. Then, the wind blows, and we are gone.

But there is a Sufi teaching, the Story of the Sand, which tells of a stream that starts in the high mountains and, after many adventures, reaches the desert. The stream feels that its destiny is to cross the desert, but as it flows into the desert sands, its water is absorbed. Crossing the desert seems impossible. The stream despairs until a voice from the sand tells it to allow itself to be raised as mist by the Sun. Then, the wind will carry it across the desert, where it will fall as rain on the other side.

Khayyam's verse is paraphrased in the second verse of Chapter Nine in this book and elaborated on in the third verse:

> Our teacher taught us what to know
> When rising from this world below.
> You wonder, dear friends
> How this story ends?
> Like water on the wind we go.

> Dry sands drink a river's flow,
> Those sparkling waters once were snow.
> Now, that journey's done.
> Raised by the Sun,
> Swiftly with the wind they go.

THE GARDEN PATH

The Afghan Sufi writer Idries Shah (1924 – 1996) tells a tale of how a nineteenth century Sufi teacher, Jan Fishan Khan, used the Ruba'iyyat as a testing device. Three young men applied to study with him. He gave each a copy of the Ruba'iyyat, telling them to read it for a week then return to tell him what they thought. A week later they returned: the first applicant said that he had been forced to think as he had never thought before. Jan Fishan accepted him as a student. The second applicant said he thought that Khayyam was a heretic. He was referred to another teacher. The third applicant said that he felt the book contained a great mystery. He was told to return after another week of study.

There is extensive argument in academic circles whether or not Khayyam was a Sufi. This is complicated because people who are not Sufis, or at least familiar with Sufi ways of thinking, have trouble saying exactly what a Sufi is. This is humorously illustrated by the entry for "Sufi" in a Persian dictionary: "Sufi chist? Sufi sufist—What is a Sufi? A Sufi is a Sufi."

Some Sufis claim that a Sufic stream has existed in all times and places; that its manifestation in the Islamic world was an adaptation to conditions of that culture. On the other side of this coin, there are Sufis who insist that no one can be a Sufi without being Muslim. Could both be correct? Sufi chist? Sufi sufist. Khayyam did not belong to any of the established Sufi Orders of his time, and there is no record of initiation so, for formalists, he is not a Sufi. He does not fit the expected box.

On the other hand, Khayyam was well-versed in Sufism in its various medieval guises, acquainted with its methods and goals, and held a favorable attitude toward it. In a metaphysical essay discussing four paths for seeking knowledge, he concludes with the remark: "The Sufis are those who do not seek knowledge intellectually or discursively, but by the cleansing of their inner self and purgation of their morals have cleansed their rational soul from the impurities of nature and the corporeal body. When that substance [the soul] is purified and becomes a reflection of the spiritual world, the forms in that status are truly unveiled without any doubt or ambiguity. This path is the best of them all.[12]"

Khayyam's writings on metaphysics, while Aristotelian and Neo-Platonic in form, show Sufi influence[13] and, when read from a Sufi perspective, the Ruba'iyyat indicates that he was intellectually and experientially familiar with Sufism. When it comes to matters of definition, terms like Sufi seem clothed in gossamer, obscured by mist, hidden by smoke and mirrors from too probing an eye, graspable only when one abandons the effort to grasp.

If a Sufi is "a Muslim mystic," as defined in a Western dictionary, then we have one understanding. On the other hand, if Sufis are those who have succeeded in cleansing their inner self and their doors of perception, then we have a different understanding. The contention that experience is what counts, that Sufism is known only by itself, begins to make sense. Perhaps it is best to forget names and look to the substance.

Who Wrote the Ruba'iyyat?

No published version of the Ruba'iyyat has been found dating earlier than a century after Khayyam's death. The number of ruba'i attributed to Khayyam, however, has grown over the centuries. Today, more than 1,400 ruba'i go under his name. Between one hundred and three hundred of these verses are accepted as written by Khayyam himself, but with few exceptions, there is no definitive resolution of authorship.

There are also questions about influences on Khayyam. Where did he get ideas? Some point to the blind Arab poet Abu'l-ala' Ma'arri as a possible source. Ma'arri was born a generation before Khayyam, wrote on similar themes and used similar images. Khayyam was familiar with and appreciated his work. Some, however, dispute that there could have been any influence. One modern scholar gives an unwitting example of assumptions that block understanding: "What can Khayyam, who is next to Avicenna in stature and is himself a mathematician and philosopher of the highest rank, learn from Abu'l-ala' Ma'arri, who was only a poet? ... Abu'l-ala' was not a philosopher or a hakim and was not even learned in philosophy.[14]"

But, what did Rumi learn from the itinerant dervish Shams? Resonance, not appearance, is what matters. In such meetings, the Spanish word *Simpaticó* best describes the nature of the connection.

SEEKING TRUTH IN DANGEROUS TIMES

For Sufis, questions of attribution and influence are not important. Khayyam is the exemplar of a school, a particular way of thought and awareness, so there will naturally be similarities, family resemblances, between his writings and others who follow the same school. Idries Shah writes, "Marri wrote like Khayyam, and Khayyam like Marri,... because they were both writing from the point of view of the same school. ...Khayyam is the Sufi voice, and the Sufi voice, to the Sufi, is timeless.[15]" Mehdi Aminrazavi says, "even though the majority of the 1400 or so Rubai'yyat are clearly inauthentic, they remain part of a literary genre that provides a consistent and coherent message.... More than a person, Khayyam is the representative of a particular worldview... The Khayyamian School represents the voices of those thinkers who for centuries have spoken through a proxy without being lynched by the orthodox.[16]"

Whether original or not, the verses attributed to Khayyam serve an instrumental function. They convey an attitude and provoke thought, undercutting any facile attempt to promote dogmatic belief or relativistic nihilism. To ask if a particular ruba'i is from Khayyam is like asking if some portion of a magnificent Renaissance painting was done by the master, or by one of his students or assistants. To presumptuously foist a new "Khayyam" verse on the existing collection,

> Fools about my dusty gravesite lurk
> Seeking secret treasures from my work.
> To make the tale clearer, I hold up a mirror—
> Whoever sees will see, if they don't shirk.

It's a case of "What we see is what we get." Readers of the Ruba'iyyat take from it what they bring to it. If this includes the ability to stretch the mind, contemplate new assumptions and defer final judgment, there is a bottomless well to draw from. People who think along pre-established channels and in terms of fixed beliefs will only see what those filters allow. What one sees in Khayyam's mirror is—oneself.

> The Teacher of the Age is near
> Imparting wisdom, bright and clear.
> What we see's the bit
> That we think will fit.
> We hear what we're prepared to hear.

Sailing for the Sun

> In every time the Truth is One,
> The Song of how a life is spun.
> Teaching true keys
> To harvest the breeze
> Sailing for the sovereign Sun.

Khayyam was a Muslim and it is an injunction for Muslims to seek knowledge. A hadith (saying of the Prophet) has it that "the best form of worship is the pursuit of knowledge." The core of Islam is the absolute unity of Allah, so "all things reveal his face." Gaining knowledge of the world, a seeker comes to God in accord with the saying: "the apparent is the bridge to the real." The goal is to recognize the divine

Unity as it manifests in creation. Seeing God in nature is a feature of all religions that see the world as the work of a divine creator. Seeking God through knowledge of the world, however, was particularly emphasized in the liberal form of Islam that flourished until the fundamentalist turn in the late tenth century of the Christian era, when free inquiry became suspect and seekers of truth fell into disrepute.

As he sought knowledge of the divine Unity, it is significant that Khayyam was a mathematician. In medieval mathematics, infinity was not a mathematical entity, but it was a concept present in theological and philosophical attempts to grasp the nature of God, referred to by Khayyam as the Necessary Being.

Fourteen centuries before, Aristotle had claimed that all change involves a move from potential to actual, and every change must have a cause. He envisioned a chain of causation and argued that to avoid infinite regress there must be an uncaused First Cause. This First Cause is the Necessary Being, the Prime Mover, eternal, unmoving, pure actuality contemplating only itself. All else is a mixture of actuality and potentiality in a state of flux as what is potential moves to become, to the extent possible, actual.

As First Cause, the Necessary Being does not cause change by contact. Rather, it is the ultimate object of love, the North Star and pole toward which all souls are oriented. All things strive to achieve full actualization in order to approach as closely as possible the perfection of pure actualized form. This is the source of the human impulse to seek truth. All humans desire knowledge, all humans are potential seekers of truth. In its highest state, the mind has fully actualized its perfection in the stillness of contemplation, a microcosmic mirror of the divine self-contemplation of the One Being.

Neo-Platonists combined this with Plato's doctrine of ideal forms and the ultimate form of the Good to say that all existence arises from the Necessary Being (the One) by emanation. When coupled with a monotheistic religion, this leads to theological problems. If God is good does this mean all good, without evil? If so, and if all things come from God, how can there be evil and suffering in the world? In the Ruba'iyyat Khayyam turns to this question again and again.

As the ultimate source the Necessary Being is unlimited, but anything said about this Being implies limitation. Hence, the Necessary Being is beyond description and conceptualization. How, then, can individuals attribute qualities to it? How does one know what is beyond the capacities of the mind to know? Any attribution imposes a limitation on the unlimited. This says something about the individual who claims to know, but not much about the Necessary Being.[17]

In modern mathematics, infinity is a topic of research. Mathematicians today realize that there are levels of infinity, rising to what is termed the *absolutely infinite*.[18] In seeking to study higher orders of the infinite, mathematicians use a reflection principle stating that anything said about the absolutely infinite is already true of some lower level of infinity. Thus, no attribution can be a description of a unique attribute of the absolutely infinite. Yet, the concept of the absolutely infinite is necessary as a foundation.

Khayyam's concept of the Necessary Being is similar. This Being cannot be described, but it is the foundation and source. Any statement made about the Necessary Being imposes limitation, hence is relative to the person making the statement. How can a person come to know God when everything they claim to know is a description of themselves? In the words of Mohammad, "who knows their self, knows their God." To know this Being, beyond subjectivity, something more is required than concepts and language—a state of consciousness beyond categorical and conceptual thought. Reaching this point, a seeker of truth must turn attention away from the external world and begin the difficult task of gaining self-knowledge, understanding that the subjective self stands as a veil masking the divine. In Sufi parlance, this is the god that must die before a person can be open to reality.

> Not you nor I can learn the inmost secret:
> The eternal Cypher proves too hard to break.
> Behind God's curtain voices babble of us
> But when it parts where then shall we two be?[19]

Speaking Truth in Dangerous Times

In a dictionary, equivocation is defined as the ambiguous use of words in order to avoid definite commitment. Like the famous Schrodinger's cat, equivocal statements contain many meanings until interpreted by an observer. In the 2009 play Equivocation,[20] William Shagspeare is commissioned to write a play about the gunpowder plot for King James to use as propaganda. While researching background for this play, Shagspeare interviewed the Jesuit priest Henry Garnet, who was arrested for participation in the plot. Garnet tells him that equivocation is "the art of telling the truth in dangerous times."

Seekers of truth recognize each other and share what they have learned, but if they want to survive, they must do so without inviting attack from the orthodox. Moreover, the important sharing is not any particular conclusion about the world, it is of secure means for investigating the world. These include skepticism of conventional beliefs, rejection of dogmatic positions, tools of reason, and tools to gain self-knowledge. Intellectual and empirical methods are important, but seeking truth with sincerity is a matter of attitude, which is difficult to transmit. It is best shown obliquely, raising questions that train a person to challenge presuppositions. Intellectual information may help, but without proper attitude, it gets in the way.

Khayyam lived in dangerous times. After four centuries of free intellectual inquiry, Islamic civilization had undergone a sea change. Strict fundamentalism and legalism dominated the social and intellectual atmosphere and Khayyam knew, by example, that were he to write anything that was seen by dogmatists as challenging the orthodox order, he would be denounced as a heretic. In such times, people become creative and posing questions, especially when done in light verses exchanged among friends, offered Khayyam a safe way to express challenges to the legalistic mullahs. The Ruba'iyyat is "not only isolated poems in which he expresses his quandary with the riddles of life, but... the response of a profound thinker who is challenging the formal opinions of orthodoxy and is able to get away with it precisely because of the poetic mode of expression he has adopted.[21]" It is a way to transmit the skeptical attitude without overly offending the orthodox.

Ruba'i are capable of multiple interpretations, giving plausible deniability if accused of heresy. They were a favorite among Persian artists, poets, and intellectuals who could use them to make comments that, if done in a less informal setting, would at best have raised an eyebrow and at worst generated accusations of atheism. A well-phrased ruba'i could serve a purpose similar to protest songs, or the kinds of humor found among populations oppressed under a tyrannical political regime, offering a safe means of expressing criticism of the powers that be. "Ruba'i could be circulated anonymously and often voiced criticism of fanatically imposed prohibitions and doctrine. The hypocrisy and lack of genuine human understanding frequently displayed by arid scholastics and wrangling religious jurisprudents were mocked. A ruba'i could be easily memorized, and as easily imitated. It could be recited in coteries of like-minded people, both for entertainment and to afford relief from oppression....[22]" The power of a ruba'i is "...in the capacity to make a short and telling statement.[23]" Yet such statements, however telling, could be dismissed as mere poetic jesting. Fundamentalists might not get the joke, or if they did, would fail to see the barb aimed in their direction.

A Hall of Mirrors

It is important to read each of Khayyam's verses with alertness to the state of consciousness being described, which is to say, the state of awareness within oneself provoked by the reading. Possible meanings drawn from one or a series of verses may hinge on how a single word is inflected. Verses 30 – 32 in the Graves-Shah translation of the Rubai'yat read:

> Man's brain has never solved the eternal Why
> Nor foraged past the frontier set for thought.
> All intellect be sure, proves nugatory,
> However hard we either teach or learn.

> In agitation I was brought to birth
> And learned nothing from life but wonder at it;
> Reluctantly we leave, still uninformed
> Why in the world we came, or went, or were.

> My presence here has been no choice of mine,
> Fate hounds me most unwillingly away.
> Rise, wrap a cloth about your loins, my Saki,
> And swill away the misery of this world.[24]

These lines seem to describe an existentialist world into which we are thrown willy nilly, where intellect, understanding, and knowledge, are impossible; a world where life is short, brutal, and meaningless. The final two lines seem to sum up this dismal condition with an exhortation to anesthetize despair with drunkenness, whether it be physical (wine) or mystical (ecstatic emotional indulgence). But, depending on how the word "this" in the final line is pronounced, with resignation or with contempt, the reference may be to the world in which we live, in which life seems to be brutal, short, and meaningless; or, it may be to the dreary and hopeless attitude that is described in the previous lines. Is the way that we see the world true, or is it colored by attitudes and emotions? Lying in the gutter, can we still appreciate the reflection of the stars in the puddle by our face?

Did Khayyam write these lines late at night after hours of futile effort to resolve a recalcitrant mathematical or metaphysical problem? Upon hearing of the death of a dear friend? Did he intend them as a comment on those who reject the world and fall into metaphysical pessimism? Did he have multiple impacts in mind? He is not here to tell us and if asked, might give one answer at one time and another at another time. He is not telling a truth but presenting possibilities, and this is so even if at the time of writing he had a definite meaning in mind. Our chosen interpretation, or our suspension of judgment, is up to us and tells us more about our own state than Khayyam's.

When asked about the meaning of a Quranic verse Khayyam would not give a single answer but offer multiple possibilities, giving pro and con arguments for each. While indicating his personal preference, he refused to endorse any interpretation as the only meaning. Contemporaries who related such tales marveled at his knowledge, but did they get anything more? Did any of those present get the point that personal choice and responsibility is always involved?

A variety of conflicting feelings follow recognition of the impossibility of any ultimate intellectual understanding of infinite reality, not because a lifetime is too short but because the tools of the intellect are inadequate. At this stage, the would-be seeker of truth is buffeted by emotional winds blowing this way and that, teetering on the brink between dogma and doubt, in danger of falling into blind belief or blind disbelief. Is Khayyam suggesting acceptance of this reality and celebration of the journey; pointing to its transformative power by virtue of which the potential of a youthful romantic visionary is alchemically transmuted into the actuality of wisdom, embodied awareness, and gratitude? The glass may be half full or half empty but the wine is good.

> Some ponder long on doctrine and belief
> Some teeter between certitude and doubt.
> Suddenly out of hiding leaps the Guide
> With: 'Fools the Way is neither that nor this.[25]

Khayyam skillfully walked the razor's edge between faith and doubt. This tells us more about him than any supposed opinion gained by interpretation of his verses. "He is too courageous and honest to accept Pascal's 'wager' and opt for the religious answer because it is 'safer,' and he is too honest to adopt Kierkegaard's view that although there is a 'risk' of being wrong in embracing faith, one must take the risk.[26]"

Rather than take an easy way out, Khayyam holds to the path between, a path that, taking the bull by the horns, "slides between the yea and nay."

Modes of Seeking

The realm of spiritual realization is far too vast for a "one size fits all" cookie cutter approach. In this garden multiple pathways meander. All paths reach the same exit, but each seeker arrives with different impressions of the journey. A way of thought is understood from the inside; to truly know one must taste, the path must be walked. Khayyam's verses have come to us on the winds of time, a transmission enriched by many others with similar outlook and temperament. He is the exemplar of a School. What worldview, what forms of thought, what system of beliefs characterize that School? What attitude binds the apparent contradictions of Khayyam's life into a unified vision?

Khayyam was a mathematician, an astronomer, a practical scientist, a philosopher who wrote essays on metaphysics. He focused his powerful intelligence on a search for ultimate understanding, stretching for the divine. He was respected as devout and religious, given the honorific title Evidence of Truth, consulted on questions of Quranic interpretation. And he wrote scandalous verses that attacked formalized religion, questioned the existence of truth, bemoaned the limits of human life and intellect, and seemed to recommend a life of either drunken dissolution, or absorption in the heady wine of emotionally indulgent mysticism. What is he exemplifying? What attitude toward the worlds of matter and spirit?

Noble Laurate Doris Lessing gives a partial answer, "To my mind the whole push and thrust and development of the world is towards the more complex, the flexible, the open-minded, the ability to entertain many ideas, sometimes contradictory ones, in one's mind at the same time.[27]" Being able to maintain contradictory ideas in mind, suspending judgment, working with what is available, being open to new information without bias, sliding between the Scylla of dogma and the Charybdis of doubt is the path of the skeptic.

Ludwig Wittgenstein quipped, "Tell me how you are searching and I will tell you what you are searching for." Any rationalistic system must fail in attempting to capture the unlimited in its net of concepts and language. For a seeker who sticks to rationalism alone, the inevitable end can only be dogmatism or relativism. Reason is the tool; it cannot be the master. Honest seekers of truth eventually reach the limits of rational thought and face a choice. Dogmatic adherence to formalism, in religion, in philosophy, in life, is to sleep and dream. Surrender to relativistic denial is to abandon the game.

Recognizing the limits of reason is not the end of the path, for the honest skeptic it only serves to indicate a new direction.

> In dim and distant days of youth
> I styled myself a mystic sleuth.
> But truths that I sought
> Were not what I got.
> It's time to learn to live in truth.

The End of the Road

"Take something with you when you go from here to there,
you show no profit if you go with empty hands."

—Omar Khayyam

Human life is finite. In this garden, all paths eventually come
to an end at a gate marked "Exit." Near the end of his life,
the great Catholic theologian Saint Thomas Aquinas, whose
work dominates Catholic theology, abandoned his writing.
According to an early biographer, this followed a vision
experienced while saying Mass on December 6, 1273. After
this shattering event Thomas said, "Such things have been
revealed to me that all that I have written seems to me as so
much straw." Giving different meanings to the word "know" in
the second and fourth lines (episteme in the second, gnosis in
the fourth), Khayyam describes a similar experience (note the
important comma in the last line):

> The desire for knowledge I could not forego
> Few secrets remained that I did not know
> For seventy-two years, I thought night and day
> Until I came to know, I had nothing to show.[28]

In some verses, Khayyam suggests that since all things are
ordered by God, life is predetermined. Although he was not
a determinist, he held that certain things are predetermined.
In two metaphysical essays, *On Being and Obligation,* and *On the
Necessity of Contradiction in the World, Determinism and Subsistence,*
he identifies three kinds of determinism: universal, socio-

economic, and ontological. Ontologically, as a human being, certain possibilities are determined, including the possibility, unique to humans, of entering into the world of mind and spirit and achieving personal realization through actualization of the innate human potential. As a social being, however, social and economic life determines the means available to attain this realization.[29] Universally, however, human beings possess free will. Whatever the conditions of a person's life, personal, moral, and ethical choices can lead to the highest possible attainment; or, at the other extreme, to failure as a human being.

> Those goods for which we have been vying
> Lose value when we see we're dying.
> It's when we get old
> We find the real gold's
> The One we've become in the trying.

It is all too easy to fall for fool's gold. To assay real gold, awareness is necessary: of the external conditions of life, of the constraints these conditions place upon freedom, and of one's internal states and capacities. Honesty is the key; trading wants and desires for real possibility. In an image used by Stoic philosophers, a dog tied to a chariot will go along whether it wills it or not. If it goes willingly, it suffers less. Within the bounds imposed by reality, a person can "take the cash and let the credit go."

Success in this work takes deep self-knowledge, something attained only through intense effort to cleanse the inner self and clarify morals and values. Jacob Bronowski tells us that we cannot know what is true unless we behave in certain ways. These ways are not found by following rules, even though following rules may be a step in the learning of them. A leap of understanding is essential: "The values by which we are to survive are not rules for just and unjust conduct, but are those deeper illuminations in whose light justice and injustice, good and evil, means and ends are seen in fearful sharpness of outline.[30]" Morality is not found in rules, it is an attitude and an achievement. "There are two things that make up morality. One is the sense that other people matter: the sense of common loyalty, of charity and tenderness, the sense of human love. The other is a clear judgment of what is at stake: a cold knowledge, without a trace of deception, of precisely what will happen to oneself and to others if one plays either the hero or the coward.[31]" Add to this the courage to accept responsibility for the consequences of one's actions.

No system of beliefs can encompass this. It is an attitude toward the world, and dedication to the work on self that allows this attitude to arise and be sustained. Being engaged in the world without being controlled by attachment to seductive attractions, beliefs, fears and desires of the world. This internal work produces a state of clarity and awareness that stands in sharp contrast to the dogmatic slumber of blind belief and the angry surrender of relativism.

Khayyam's position in society was determined and he fulfilled his allotted role with integrity and brilliance. His verses were a socially acceptable channel of expression that he used to subvert fixed dogmas, undermine rigid beliefs, and transmit the skeptical attitude. But he was no atheist. He exemplifies the only state in which true faith is possible—a state in which the reasoning mind, accepting that it does not and cannot know ultimate truth, still remains open, seeking to drain one last drop from the cup, transmuting knowledge and experience into wisdom and gratitude. In this state, consciousness stands at the fulcrum of the two worlds, delicately balancing the sensory world and the world of mind and spirit, receptive to illumination from the divine.

> A finger pointing at the Moon
> Reasons task and reasons boon.
> Our guiding light
> Through darkest night,
> Heralding Sunrise is soon.

Categorization, classification, systems of assumptions and postulates, the internal structures of ego may be necessary for functional purposes, but insisting that any conceptual system reveals ultimate truth produces attachment to a limiting view of reality. The individual person, the ego and personality, serves as a steward operating under the direction of a higher awareness that can only manifest in full when the veils of self are lifted. This takes watchfulness guided by reason, and faith that the internal compass is true, that the guiding orientation, the North Star for action, is love.

As Socrates lay dying, he told friends that he looked forward to entering the Elysian Fields where he could question famous figures of the past. He said that although he did not know if this picture of an afterlife was true, he chose it because he liked it. In the relative world of the individual self, Khayyam was a mathematician, astronomer, philosopher, and scandalous poet, following the skeptical path. But he was also a Muslim and there is no doubting the sincerity of his final prayer: "O God, Thou are aware that I have known Thee to the full extent of my powers. Forgive me, for my knowledge of Thee is my way of coming to Thee."

> I saw a mystic stranger who gave no heed
> For caste or creed, for faith or worldly greed.
> And free from truth and quest, from path and goal,
> He sat at ease, from Earth and Heaven freed.[32]

Endnotes

[1] This tale is elaborated in extensive detail in The Book of the Book by Idries Shah.

[2] Robert Graves and Omar Ali Shah (trans.) The Rubaiyyat of Omar Khayyam, p.54.

[3] Muggles, to use a word from Harry Potter.

[4] The essay The Lure of Syracuse by Mark Lilla gives a detailed study of the sort of trouble that can face philosophers who fall under the spell of eros.

[5] From The Wine of Wisdom, p.55

[6] The Ruba'iyyt of Omar Khayyam, translated by Edward FitzGerald, p.39.

[7] Arthur Lovejoy, The Great Chain of Being.

[8] From The Wine of Wisdom, p.71.

[9] Mehdi Aminrazavi, The Wine of Wisdom, p.69.

[10] Translated by Mehdi Aminrazavi in The Wine of Wisdom, p.82.

[11] Robert Graves and Omar Ali Shah (trans.) The Rubaiyyat of Omar Khayyam, p.50.

[12] Quote from The Wine of Wisdom, p.136.

[13] This is a two-sided issue since medieval Sufi thought was strongly influenced by Neo-Platonism.

[14] Quoted in The Wine of Wisdom, p.88.

[15] The Sufis, p.187.

[16] The Wine of Wisdom, p.98.

[17] Khayyam's contemporary, the brilliant Islamic theologian Muhammad al Ghazali, gives a classification of levels of understanding of God along these lines in his work Niche for Lights.

[18] The simplest example of different levels of infinity is between the infinity of counting numbers and the set of real numbers. Gregor Cantor proved this using a "diagonal slash" argument: imagine that these two infinite sets are equal in size. Then it will be possible to count the real numbers, hence (at least in principle) make a list starting with the first and going on from there, writing each real number out in decimal form. Consider the k-th number in the list, look at its k-th digit and change it to some other digit. Now consider the number we get by reading down the diagonal of the list. It cannot be contained in the list because it differs from every other number in the list in at least one digit. But we have assumed that the list contains all real numbers! Therefore, there are more real numbers than there are counting numbers, the real numbers cannot be counted.

[19] Robert Graves and Omar Ali Shah (trans.) The Rubaiyyat of Omar Khayyam.

[20] Bill Cain (2009) Equivocation.

[21] The Wine of Wisdom, p.87.

[22] Peter Avery and John Heath-Stubbs (trans.) The Ruba'iyat of Omar Khayyam. P.23.

[23] Peter Avery and John Heath-Stubbs (trans.), The Ruba'iyat of Omar Khayyam, p.10.

[24] Robert Graves and Omar Ali Shah, The Rubaiyyat of Omar Khayyam.

[25] Robert Graves and Omar Ali Shah (trans.) The Rubaiyyat of Omar Khayyam.

[26] From The Wine of Wisdom, p.133.

[27] Doris Lessing (1985) Prisons We Choose to Live Inside, p.72.

[28] The Wine of Wisdom, p.103, Mehdi Aminrazavi (trans.)

[29] A person who must work to support a family cannot spend years meditating in a cave, even if that were known to be an effective method of spiritual development.

[30] Jacob Bronowski, Science and Human Values. p.94.

[31] Jacob Bronowski, A Sense of the Future, p.205.

[32] From The Wine of Wisdom, p.74. This translation, and the Avery and Heath-Stubbs translation from the front page are the same ruba'i.

Resources

The Khayyam verses quoted here come from Mehdi Aminrazavi's translations in The Wine of Wisdom, from the Edward FitzGerald translation, and from the Robert Graves & Omar Ali Shah translation of the Ruba'iyat. Much of the historical information is drawn from The Wine of Wisdom, which is an excellent introduction to Khayyam, his times, his thought, and differing responses to his Ruba'iyat under differing social and cultural conditions.

Medhi Aminrazavi (2007) The Wine of Wisdom. Oxford: Oneworld.

Robert Arnot, Edward FitzGerald, E.H. Winfield, and J.B. Nicolas (1903) The Sufistic Quatrains of Omar Khayyam. London: M. Walter Dunne.

Peter Avery and John Heath-Stubbs (1981) The Ruba'iyat of Omar Khayyam. London: Penguin.

Jacob Bronowski (1956) Science and Human Values. NY: Julian Messner.

Jacob Bronowski (1978) A Sense of the Future. Cambridge, MA: MIT Press.

Edward FitzGerald (1967) The Rubáiyádt of Omar Khayyam. NY: Avon.

Swami Govinda Tirtha (1941) The Nectar of Grace: Omar Khayyam's Life and Works. Bombay, India: Government Central Press.

Robert Graves and Omar Ali Shah (1972) The Rubaiyat of Omar Khayyam. Harmondsworth: Penguin.

Wes Jamroz (2018) A Journey with Omar Khayyam. Montreal: Troubadour.

Doris Lessing (1987) Prisons We Choose to Live Inside. NY: Harper and Row.

Arthur O. Lovejoy (1993) The Great Chain of Being. Cambridge, MA: Harvard University Press.

Al-Ma'arri (2015) Paul Smith (trans.) The Book of al-Ma'arri. Amazon.

Rudy Rucker (1982) Infinity and the Mind. Princeton: Princeton University Press.

J.E. Saklatwalla (1978) Omar Khayyam as a Mystic. St. Paul, MN: R. West.

Idries Shah (1971) The Sufis. NY: Anchor.

Mark Twain (1983) Mark Twain's Rubáiyát. B. MacDonnell and Alan Gribben (eds.) Austin, TX, Jenkins.

Paramahansa Yogananda (1994) Wine of the Mystic: The "Rubáyát of Omar Khayyam. Los Angeles: Self-Realization Fellowship.

Eben Francis Thompson (1967) The Wisdom of Omar Khayyam. NY: Citadel.

CPSIA information can be obtained
at www.ICGtesting.com
Printed in the USA
BVHW030825290322
632741BV00001B/47